For Black Boys W
Suicide When the

Ryan Ca

methuen | drama
LONDON • NEW YORK • OXFORD • NEW DELHI • SYDNEY

METHUEN DRAMA
Bloomsbury Publishing Plc
50 Bedford Square, London, WC1B 3DP, UK
1385 Broadway, New York, NY 10018, USA
29 Earlsfort Terrace, Dublin 2, Ireland

BLOOMSBURY, METHUEN DRAMA and the Methuen
Drama logo are trademarks of Bloomsbury Publishing Plc

First published in Great Britain 2021

This edition published 2022
Reprinted 2022

A catalogue record for this book is available from the British Library.

A catalog record for this book is available from the Library of Congress.

ISBN: PB: 978-1-3503-4063-3
ePDF: 978-1-3503-4064-0
ePub: 978-1-3503-4065-7

Series: Modern Plays

Typeset by Mark Heslington Ltd, Scarborough, North Yorkshire
Printed and bound in Great Britain

To find out more about our authors and books visit
www.bloomsbury.com and sign up for our newsletters.

THE ROYAL COURT THEATRE PRESENTS
IN ASSOCIATION WITH NEW DIORAMA THEATRE & NOUVEAU RICHE

For Black Boys Who Have Considered Suicide When The Hue Gets Too Heavy

By Ryan Calais Cameron

For Black Boys Who Have Considered Suicide When The Hue Gets Too Heavy was commissioned by New Diorama Theatre and co-commissioned by Boundless Theatre.

For Black Boys Who Have Considered Suicide When The Hue Gets Too Heavy was first performed at New Diorama Theatre on Tuesday 12 October 2021 and at the Royal Court Jerwood Theatre Downstairs, Sloane Square, on Thursday 31 March 2022.

For Black Boys Who Have Considered Suicide When The Hue Gets Too Heavy

By Ryan Calais Cameron

CAST (in alphabetical order)

Onyx **Mark Akintimehin**
Pitch **Emmanuel Akwafo**
Jet **Nnabiko Ejimofor**
Sable **Darragh Hand**
Obsidian **Aruna Jalloh**
Midnight **Kaine Lawrence**

Written & Directed by **Ryan Calais Cameron**
Co-Director & Original Director **Tristan Fynn-Aiduenu**
Designer **Anna Reid**
Lighting Designer **Rory Beaton**
Sound Designer **Nicola T. Chang**
Movement Director **Theophilus O. Bailey - Godson**
Musical Director & Vocal Coach **John Pfumojena**
Assistant Director **Monaé Robinson**
Associate Sound Designer **Jahmiko Marshall**
Production Dramatherapist **Wabriya King**
Production Manager **Sayeedah Supersad**
Stage Manager **Marie-Angelique St. Hill**
Deputy Stage Manager **Mica Taylor**
Assistant Stage Manager **Stacey Nurse**
Set built by **Royal Court Stage Department & Ridiculous Solutions**

From the Royal Court, on this production:

Company Manager **Joni Carter**
Stage Supervisor **Steve Evans**
Lead Producer **Jasmyn Fisher-Ryner**
Outreach Co-ordinator **Isaac O'Connor-Adekoya**
Lighting Supervisor **Eimante Rukaite**
Lighting Programmer **Stephen Settle**
Costume Supervisor **Lucy Walshaw**

The Royal Court Theatre and Stage Management wish to thank the following for their help with this production:
Tawanda Mapanda (saxophonist), Cat Padgham (DSM).

For Black Boys Who Have Considered Suicide When The Hue Gets Too Heavy

By Ryan Calais Cameron

Ryan Calais Cameron
(Writer & Director)

For the Royal Court: **Living Newspaper, My White Best Friend (and Other Letters Left Unsaid).**

As writer, other theatre includes: **Human Nurture** (Theatre Centre/Crucible, Sheffield/UK tour); **For Black Boys Who Have Considered Suicide When the Hue Gets Too Heavy** (Nouveau Riche/Boundless/New Diorama); **Queens of Sheba** [co-writer] (Nouveau Riche/Edinburgh Festival Fringe/New Diorama/UK tour); **Typical** (Nouveau Riche/Edinburgh Festival Fringe/Soho); **Rhapsody** (Arcola); **Timbuktu** (Black Lives Black Words Festival, Bush/Theatre Royal, Stratford East).

Awards include: **Edinburgh Untapped Award, The Stage Edinburgh Award, Offie Award for Best Performance Piece** (Queens of Sheba), **Off West End Adopt A Playwright Award** (Rhapsody).

Ryan is the Co-Founder and Artistic Director of Nouveau Riche Theatre Company.

Mark Akintimehin (Onyx)

Theatre includes: **For Black Boys Who Have Considered Suicide When the Hue Gets Too Heavy** (Nouveau Riche/Boundless/New Diorama); **Excluded** (Intermission Youth Theatre); **Shakespeare Within the Abbey** (Globe); **Tribal** (2far Media); **Anansi & the London Girl** (Project 1957).

Media includes: **Somewhere in London** [web series].

Film includes: **Little Monster** [short].

Emmanuel Akwafo (Pitch)

Theatre includes: **For Black Boys Who Have Considered Suicide When the Hue Gets Too Heavy** (Nouveau Riche/Boundless/New Diorama); **Whisper Me** (Dugdale); **The Bald Soprano** (Out of the Box); **Can't Pay? Won't Pay!** (Windsor); **The Spalding Suite** (Southbank); **Scenes from the Ecstatic Bible, The Bacchae** (Melton)

Television includes: **The Crown, 24: Live Another Day, Switch, The Surgery: MTV, Grange Hill.**

Film includes: **Now You See Me 2, Tarzan, Breaking the Bank, Set the Thames on Fire.**

Theophilus O. Bailey – Godson
(Movement Director)

Theophilus is a hip hop dancer and choreographer who pioneers krump in the UK. A senior member of Boy Blue and a *Got To Dance* Finalist for Sky 1, he has danced and choreographed for FKA Twigs, Fergie, Giggs, Swizz Beatz, Dua Lipa and Little Mix, among others. He is currently a resident cast member of Channing Tatum's *Magic Mike Live* and was movement director for Boy Better Know's *Athlete* music video. Theophilus continues to choreograph and direct work, including *The Blood of Macbeth, Enter the Raw* and *Energysquad*, which is currently still in development.

Theophilus worked with Kenrick 'H20' Sandy as an assistant dance captain and performer for the Opening Ceremony of the London 2012 Olympics, and was a cast member of the Laurence Olivier Award-nominated *Blak Whyte Gray* which continues to tour internationally.

Rory Beaton (Lighting Designer)

Theatre includes: **Spike, Kiss Me Kate** (Watermill); I Love You, You're Perfect, Now Change! (Coliseum/Broadway); Lovely Ugly City (Almeida); Dishoom!, Maklena, Skylight (UK Tour); Summer Holiday, The Rise & Fall of Little Voice (Octagon, Bolton); Edward II (Arts, Cambridge); West End Producer – Free Willy! (Cuffe & Taylor); 60 Miles by Road or Rail (Theatre Royal, Northampton); Tumble Tuck (King's Head); The Blonde Bombshells of 1943, Summer Holiday, A Christmas Carol (Pitlochry Festival); How Love is Spelt (Southwark); A Christmas Carol (Belgrade, Coventry/Chipping Norton); Mysterious Bruises, Spring Awakening (RADA); Boat, The Best Day Ever (Company3); Betty Blue Eyes (Trinity Laban); Tell Us Who We Are (Y-Dance Scotland); Dumbledore is so Gay (& Pleasance), 4 (Vaults).

Opera includes: **Macbeth, La Bohème, Elizabeth I,** Dido & Aeneas, Amadigi, Il Tabarro, Idomeneo, Jonas, The Golden Cockerel, Gianni Schicchi, The Marriage of Figaro, Radamisto (English Touring Opera); Dubliners (Opera Theatre Company, Dublin); L'incoronazione di Poppea ((Trinity Laban); Così fan Tutte, The Little Green Swallow (Guildhall); Hansel & Gretel, Le Nozze di Figaro (Royal College of Music); Little Women, L'amico Fritz, The Cunning Little Vixen, Così fan Tutte, L'arlesiana, Manon Lescaut, Le Nozze di Figaro (Opera Holland Park); 70 Års Opera (Danish National Opera); Der Freischütz (Blackheath Community Opera); Rigoletto, La Scala di Seta,

Riders to the Sea, Il Campanello, The Bear
(Wexford Festival Opera).

Awards include: **Michael Northen Award
(Association of Lighting Designers)**.

Nicola T. Chang (Sound Designer)

For the Royal Court: **White Pearl.**

Theatre includes: **All Mirth and No Matter (RSC);
Dziady/Forefather's Eve (Almeida); The Death of
Ophelia (Sam Wanamaker); 15 Heroines (Jermyn
Street/Digital Theatre); Miss Julie (Chester
Storyhouse); Wild Goose Dreams (Theatre Royal,
Bath); Little Baby Jesus (Orange Tree); Summer
Rolls (Park); No Man's Land (Square Chapel,
Halifax); A Hundred Words for Snow (Arcola).**

As performer/musician, theatre includes: **SIX (West End);
STOMP! (West End/International tour).**

Nicola is a composer and sound designer for
stage and screen. She is a member of the
2020/21 Old Vic 12 cohort, the BFI x BAFTA Crew
and a Composer/Musical Director attached to
British Youth Music Theatre UK. She was co-
winner of the Evening Standard Future Theatre
Fund (Audio Design) in 2021.

Nicola has performed with the Chineke!
Orchestra, the Women of the World Orchestra
and the London Film Music Orchestra, and at
venues such as the Royal Albert Hall, Royal
Festival Hall and Shakespeare's Globe. In 2017,
she conducted the London Film Music Orchestra
playing her original soundtrack to *The Perfect
Dinner* accompanied by a live film screening,
and premiered her concerto for Ping Pong
and Piano Trio at the Queen Elizabeth Hall in
January 2019, and in Shanghai later that year.

Nnabiko Ejimofor (Jet)

Theatre includes: **For Black Boys Who Have
Considered Suicide When the Hue Gets
Too Heavy (Nouveau Riche/Boundless/New
Diorama).**

Radio includes: **Sarah Walker's Sunday Morning
Show.**

Film includes: **Attercoppe [short], Tingles [short],
Figure [short].**

Nnabiko has previously been a dancer for Boy
Blue Entertainment.

Tristan Fynn–Aiduenu
(Co-Director & Original Director)

As director, theatre includes: **Sundown Kiki (Young
Vic); For Black Boys Who Have Considered
Suicide When the Hue Gets Too Heavy (Nouveau
Riche/Boundless/New Diorama); Little Baby
Jesus (Orange Tree); Twilight (St. Mary's
University); The Spalding Suite (LAMDA); Gone
Too Far! (Guildhall).**

As writer/director, theatre includes: **Sweet Like
Chocolate Boy (Jack Studio/BAC/Tobacco
Factory/Theatre Peckham).**

As assistant director, theatre includes: **The Brothers
Size (Young Vic).**

Awards include: **2019 JMK Young Director Award.**

Darragh Hand (Sable)

Theatre includes: **For Black Boys Who Have
Considered Suicide When the Hue Gets
Too Heavy (Nouveau Riche/Boundless/New
Diorama).**

Aruna Jalloh (Obsidian)

Theatre includes: **Much Ado About Nothing (RSC);
For Black Boys Who Have Considered Suicide
When the Hue Gets Too Heavy (Nouveau Riche/
Boundless/New Diorama); Impact, Could Never
Be Me (Little Fish); Glockenspiel (Old Sole).**

Media includes: **C Biz: Obsession [music video].**

Wabriya King
(Production Dramatherapist)

For the Royal Court: **Is God Is, seven methods of
killing kylie jenner.**

Other theatre includes: **Red Pitch, Old Bridge, 10
Nights, Overflow, Pink Lemonade, Lava, The High
Table (Bush); Rockets & Blue Lights (National);
Can I Live? (Complicite); Get Up Stand Up! The
Bob Marley Musical (West End); White Noise
(Bridge); Queens of Sheba, Curious, Shuck
n Jive, TYPICAL (Soho); For Black Boys Who
Have Considered Suicide When the Hue Gets
Too Heavy (Nouveau Riche/Boundless/New
Diorama); Love and Other Acts of Violence
(Donmar); Blue/Orange (Royal & Derngate,
Northampton); The Merchant of Venice, Romeo
& Juliet (Globe); Little Scratch, The Death of a
Black Man (Hampstead); Sessions, May Queen,
Black Love (Paines Plough); 846 Live (Theatre
Royal, Stratford East).**

Wabriya graduated as an actress from The
Oxford School of Drama in 2012 and qualified
with an MA in Dramatherapy from the
University of Roehampton in 2019. She is the
Associate Dramatherapist at the Bush Theatre
supporting staff and productions.

Kaine Lawrence (Midnight)

Theatre includes: **For Black Boys Who Have Considered Suicide When the Hue Gets Too Heavy (Nouveau Riche/Boundless/New Diorama)**.

Jahmiko Marshall
(Associate Sound Designer)

As sound designer, theatre includes: **Parliament Square, Desert Boy, The Light (LAMDA)**.

As assistant lighting designer, theatre includes: **Boy (LAMDA)**.

As chief electrician/programmer, theatre includes: **Spalding Suite, Love & Information, Junkyard (LAMDA)**.

Jahmiko is a Lighting and Sound Designer from Bermuda. He obtained his Lighting Technology Certificate from Stagecraft Institute of Las Vegas and is currently a student at LAMDA studying towards his BA Hons in Production and Technical Arts.

Stacey Nurse
(Assistant Stage Manager)

As production manager, theatre includes: **When This Is Over (New Diorama)**.

As assistant production manager, theatre includes: **Dance No2° (The Place)**.

As assistant stage manager, other theatre includes: **For Black Boys Who Have Considered Suicide When the Hue Gets Too Heavy (New Diorama)**.

After training in Dance at the University of Roehampton, Stacey fell in love with technical theatre and went on to train as a technician at the London Contemporary Dance School and The Place Theatre. They are currently working within the freelance production and lighting design worlds. Stacey also manages the technical and production aspects of queer/POC-run arts collective COARSEN.

John Pfumojena
(Musical Director & Vocal Coach)

As composer/musical director, theatre includes: **The Jungle (Good Chance/Young Vic/West End/St Ann's, NYC/Curran, San Francisco); Volpone, Dr. Faustus (Tangle/UK tour); Junk Yard (LAMDA)**.

As performer, theatre includes: **The Jungle (Good Chance/Young Vic/West End/St Ann's, NYC/Curran, San Francisco)**.

Discography includes: **Sounds of Refuge (John Falsetto & Mohamed Sarrar); Phoenix Rise (Sunny Jain, John Falsetto as featuring composer and artist)**.

Awards include: **BroadwayWorld Award San Francisco for Best Featured Actor in a Play, OBIE Special Citation Award NYC (The Jungle)**;

Honorary (Cultural Ambassador) Zimbabwe Achievers Award UK; Panel's Choice Award (Actor/Musician); Young Achievers Award, Zimbabwe.

John Pfumojena (aka John Falsetto) is a Zimbabwean Mbira and Marimba Virtuoso, composer, vocalist, actor and director. He has been an active creative for 23 years and has toured many countries in Africa, South America, North America, Europe and Asia, sharing stages and festival billing with African juggernauts such as Oliver Mtukudzi, Salif Keita, Chiwoniso Maraire, Baaba Mal and Angelique Kidjo. Festival appearances include Victorious, Shambala and Journeys Festivals in the UK, Harare International Festival of the Arts (Zimbabwe), 2nd PanAfrican Festival of Algiers (Algeria), Poetry Festival Konstanz (Germany) and Mwezi Wawala Festival (Malawi).

John is a Visiting Fellow of the University of Oxford, a composer/songwriter with Warner Chappell Music (Warner Music Group), an Associate Artist at Tangle Theatre Company, a Jerwood Live Work Fund Recipient 2021 and a Professional Member of The Ivors Academy.

Anna Reid (Designer)

Theatre includes: **For Black Boys Who Have Considered Suicide When the Hue Gets Too Heavy (Nouveau Riche/Boundless/New Diorama); The Memory Of Water, Sleepwalking, Cash Cow, Paradise, The Hoes (Hampstead); Sessions (Paines Plough/Soho); Dust (New York Theatre Workshop/Soho); Four Minutes Twelve Seconds, The Kitchen Sink, Jumpers For Goalposts (Oldham Coliseum); Late Night Staring At High Res Pixels, Scrounger, I'm Gonna Pray For You So Hard (Finborough); The Sweet Science Of Bruising (Wilton's Music Hall); Our Country's Good, A Midsummer Night's Dream (Tobacco Factory); Twelfth Night, Collective Rage, Dear Brutus, The Cardinal, School Play (Southwark); Soft Animals, Fury (Soho); Mary's Babies, Dry Land (Jermyn Street); Rasheeda Speaking (Trafalgar Studios); Schism (Park); Grotty (Bunker); Tiny Dynamite (Old Red Lion); Rattle Snake (Live, Newcastle/Theatre Royal, York/Soho); Sex Worker's Opera [set design] (Compagnietheater, Amsterdam/ National tour); Arthur's World (Bush); Hippolytos (V&A Museum); Hamlet (Riverside Studios)**.

Opera includes: **Opera Double Bill – Judith Weir's Miss Fortune and Menotti's The Telephone (Guildhall)**.

Anna was selected to represent the UK as an emerging designer at World Stage Design in Taipei.

Monaé Robinson
(Assistant Director)

As director, theatre includes: **OJA [Young, Gifted and Black Festival] (Theatre Peckham).**

As assistant director, theatre includes: **Red Pitch (Bush).**

Monaé started off her career as a community and cultural arts leader, and is a performance maker that typically focuses on Afrofuturism. She is the recipient of the Resident Director Bursary programme at the Bush Theatre and was named one of Alfred Fagon's 25 Black leaders in theatre. Monaé holds a Bachelor's degree in Theatre & Performance from Goldsmiths University.

Marie-Angelique St. Hill
(Stage Manager)

As assistant stage manager, for the Royal Court: **A Kind of People.**

As stage manager, theatre includes: **Trojan Horse [rehearsals] (LUNG); 5 Plays (Young Vic).**

As assistant stage manager, other theatre includes: **Tree (& Manchester International Festival), Hamlet (Young Vic); Aladdin, Cinderella (Hackney Empire); In the Night Garden Live (National tour).**

Sayeedah Supersad
(Production Manager)

As stage manager, for the Royal Court: **Living Newspaper, Listen Local.**

As assistant stage manager, for the Royal Court: **Rare Earth Mettle, ear for eye, Goats, Father Comes Home from the Wars.**

As production manager, theatre includes: **Passion Fruit, For Black Boys Who Have Considered Suicide When the Hue Gets Too Heavy (New Diorama).**

As stage manager, other theatre includes: **Land Without Dreams (Gate).**

As assistant stage manager, other theatre includes: **Death of a Salesman (Young Vic); Paradise (Hampstead); Utility (Orange Tree); Mapping Brent Festival (Kiln); Sinbad the Sailor (Theatre Royal, Stratford East); Umm Kulthum and the Golden Era (London Palladium).**

Mica Taylor (Deputy Stage Manager)

As stage manager, for the Royal Court: **Is God Is, seven methods of killing kylie jenner, Living Newspaper.**

As stage manager, other theatre includes: **Trouble in Mind (National).**

As deputy stage manager, other theatre includes: **Girls (HighTide/Talawa/Soho/Tour); Cuttin' It (Young Vic/Tour).**

As assistant stage manager, theatre includes: **Manor, Master Harold, Small Island, St George and the Dragon(National); Obsession (Barbican/International tour); Sleeping Beauty (Hackney Empire).**

As assistant stage manager/art department, music videos include: **Yesterday (Loyle Carner).**

THE ROYAL COURT THEATRE

The Royal Court Theatre is the writers' theatre. It is a leading force in world theatre for cultivating and supporting writers – undiscovered, emerging and established.

Through the writers, the Royal Court is at the forefront of creating restless, alert, provocative theatre about now. We open our doors to the unheard voices and free thinkers that, through their writing, change our way of seeing.

Over 120,000 people visit the Royal Court in Sloane Square, London, each year and many thousands more see our work elsewhere through transfers to the West End and New York, UK and international tours, digital platforms, our residencies across London, and our site-specific work. Through all our work we strive to inspire audiences and influence future writers with radical thinking and provocative discussion.

The Royal Court's extensive development activity encompasses a diverse range of writers and artists and includes an ongoing programme of writers' attachments, readings, workshops and playwriting groups. Twenty years of the International Department's pioneering work around the world means the Royal Court has relationships with writers on every continent.

Since 1956 we have commissioned and produced hundreds of writers, from John Osborne to Jasmine Lee-Jones. Royal Court plays from every decade are now performed on stage and taught in classrooms and universities across the globe.

We're now working to the future and are committed to becoming carbon net zero and ensuring we are a just, equitable, transparent and ethical cultural space - from our anti-oppression work, to our relationship with freelancers, to credible climate pledges.

It is because of this commitment to the writer and our future that we believe there is no more important theatre in the world than the Royal Court.

**Find out more at
royalcourttheatre.com**

 royalcourt  royalcourttheatre

Supported using public funding by
**ARTS COUNCIL
ENGLAND**

ROYAL

ASSISTED PERFORMANCES

Captioned Performances

Captioned performances are accessible for people who are D/deaf, deafened & hard of hearing, as well as being suitable for people for whom English is not a first language.

For Black Boys Who Have Considered Suicide When The Hue Gets Too Heavy: Wed 20 April, Wed 27 April, 7.30pm
two Palestinians go dogging: Fri 27 May, 7.45pm

BSL-interpreted Performance

BSL-interpreted performances, delivered by an interpreter, give a sign interpretation of the text spoken and/or sung by artists in the onstage production

Audio-described Performances

Audio-described performances are accessible for people who are blind or partially sighted. They are preceded by a touch tour which allows patrons access to elements of theatre design including set and costume.

For Black Boys Who Have Considered Suicide When The Hue Gets Too Heavy: Sat 30 April, 2.30pm

COURT

ASSISTED PERFORMANCES

Performances in a Relaxed Environment

Relaxed Environment performances are suitable for those who may benefit from a more relaxed environment.

During these performances:

– There is a relaxed attitude to noise in the auditorium; you are welcome to respond to the show in whatever way feels natural
– You can enter and exit the auditorium when needed
– We will help you find the best seats for your experience
– House lights may remain raised slightly
– Loud noises may be reduced

For Black Boys Who Have Considered Suicide When The Hue Gets Too Heavy: Sat 23 April, 2.30pm
two Palestinians go dogging: Sat 28 May, 3pm

If you would like to talk to us about your access requirements, please contact our Box Office at (0)20 7565 5000 or boxoffice@royalcourttheatre.com
The Royal Court Visual Story is available on our website. We also produce Story and Sensory synopses which are available on request.

 New
Diorama
Theatre

New Diorama Theatre is a pioneering studio venue in the heart of London.

Based on the corner of Regent's Park, over the last 10 years New Diorama has been the home of a new movement in British theatre, supporting the country's best independent companies and ensembles. Our commissions and productions frequently tour and transfer nationally and internationally, including regular seasons Off-Broadway.

'A must-visit destination for London theatregoers' Time Out

In February 2022, New Diorama was named Fringe Theatre of the Year at the Stage Awards, the second time the venue has won that award in its short history. New Diorama has also previously won three Peter Brook Awards, seven OffWestEnd Awards, OffWestEnd Artistic Director of the Year, and The Stage's Innovation Prize. The Stage 100 currently list New Diorama as the UK's most influential studio theatre.

A genuine theatrical phenomenon... An unfunded miniature powerhouse' The Stage, Feb 2022

Our community programme reaches 11,000+ people across our local area every year, from original commissions touring school and community venues, to our Camden Youth Theatre, and a partnership with Third Age Project, hosting special events for isolated and elderly residents.

'A crucial part of the wider UK theatre ecology and an under-sung hero' Guardian

In 2021, New Diorama opened the revolutionary NDT Broadgate, a brand new 20,000 square foot rehearsal and development complex offered entirely free to independent artists to support post-Covid recovery. *For Black Boys Who Have Considered Suicide When The Hue Gets Too Heavy* was one of the first shows made at NDT Broadgate, where Nouveau Riche are also an Associate Company.

'New Diorama has only been around for a decade but has already left a huge mark on the global theatre scene' WhatsOnStage

www.newdiorama.com / @newdiorama

New
Diorama
Theatre

"Nouveau Riche are UK's most exciting new theatre company, with their previous 'Queens of Sheba' hitting perfection."

To Do List London

Nouveau Riche is a multi-award-winning creative movement, aiming to discover and produce unique stories with a keen scope on work that is both educational and entertaining. We have set out to create and nurture new writing that is thought provoking, challenging and culturally inclusive.

The most common theme in our work is that we tend to depart from traditional Western storytelling, experimenting with fresh, contemporary, and unconventional methods. Our mission is to programme shows and events of the highest possible quality and to develop new ways of engaging audiences and artists.

Our hit show 'Queens of Sheba' won The Stage Edinburgh Festival Award 2018, Edinburgh Untapped Award 2018 and Best Performance Piece – Off-West End Awards 2020.

"After 10 years of writing and developing 'For Black Boys' it was remarkable to experience these stories at NDT. This transfer will be a huge landmark for Nouveau Riche and our community, to see the words 'For Black Boys' in bright lights in the centre of Sloane Square."

Ryan Calais Cameron

nvrch.com
@nvrch

Nouveau Riche

Co-Founder & Artistic Director	Ryan Calais Cameron
Co-Founder	Shavani Cameron
Producer	Sarah Jordan Verghese
Associate Director	Ewa Dina
Creative Producer	Joshua Boyd-Campbell
Creative Producer	Jacob Roberts-Mensah

boundless theatre

"It's the best play I've seen this year to articulate an urgent contemporary moment." *****
(The Metro on *Natives*, a Boundless Theatre production)

Since 2001 Boundless Theatre has supported a community of young adults to be creative. The work is exhilarating, shareable and promotes meaningful social experiences around culture. Boundless is in dialogue with a vibrant and diverse youth culture. By investing in and being inspired by early career artists we promote conversation with a global community of 15–25-year-olds.

Launching in 2022, the Boundless Drama Club is a UK wide network and creative community that will act as an introduction to theatre making and a resource for developing new creative relationships and skills. Making the most of online learning, real time, digital experiences and in time creative commissions and financial support for work, the Boundless Drama Club will sit at the centre of all our artistic development and creative community work.

The development of *For Black Boys Who Have Considered Suicide When The Hue Gets Too Heavy* was supported through Boundless Accelerator, a creative development programme from Boundless Theatre funded by the Garfield Weston Foundation.

boundlesstheatre.org.uk
@boundlessabound

ROYAL COURT SUPPORTERS

The Royal Court relies on its supporters in addition to our core grant from Arts Council England and our ticket sales. We are particularly grateful to the individuals, trusts and companies who stood by us and continued to support our work during these recent difficult times. It is with this vital support that the Royal Court remains the writers' theatre and that we can continue to seek out, develop and nurture new voices, both on and off our stages.

Thank you to all who support the Royal Court in this way. We really can't do it without you.

PUBLIC FUNDING

Supported using public funding by
**ARTS COUNCIL
ENGLAND**

CHARITABLE PARTNERS

BackstageTrust

**JERWOOD
ARTS**

ORANGE TREE
TRUST

CORPORATE SPONSORS

Aqua Financial Ltd
Cadogan
Colbert
Edwardian Hotels, London
SISTER

CORPORATE MEMBERS

Platinum
Auriens
Bloomberg Philanthropies

Silver
Left Bank Pictures
Patrizia
Sloane Stanley

TRUSTS & FOUNDATIONS

The Derrill Allatt Foundation
The Backstage Trust
Martin Bowley Charitable Trust
The City Bridge Trust
The Cleopatra Trust
Cockayne – Grants for the Arts
The Noël Coward Foundation
Cowley Charitable Foundation
The D'Oyly Carte Charitable Trust
Edgerton Foundation
Garrick Charitable Trust
The Golden Bottle Trust
Roderick & Elizabeth Jack
Jerwood Arts
Kirsh Foundation
The London Community Foundation
Clare McIntyre's Bursary
Lady Antonia Fraser for the Pinter Commission
Old Possum's Practical Trust
Richard Radcliffe Charitable Trust
Rose Foundation
Royal Victoria Hall Foundation
The Charles Skey Charitable Trust
John Thaw Foundation
Thistle Trust
The Victoria Wood Foundation

To find out more about supporting the Royal Court please get in touch with the Development Team at support@royalcourttheatre.com, call 020 7565 5030 or visit royalcourttheatre.com/support-us

The English Stage Company at the Royal Court is a registered charity (No. 231242)

ROYAL

BAR & KITCHEN

The Royal Court's Bar & Kitchen aims to create a welcoming and inspiring environment with a style and ethos that reflects the work we put on stage.

Offering expertly crafted cocktails alongside an extensive selection of craft gins and beers, wine and soft drinks, our vibrant basement bar provides a sanctuary in the middle of Sloane Square. By day a perfect spot for meetings or quiet reflection and by night atmospheric meeting spaces for cast, crew, audiences and the general public.

All profits go directly to supporting the work of the Royal Court theatre, cultivating and supporting writers – undiscovered, emerging and established.

For more information, visit
royalcourttheatre.com/bar

HIRES & EVENTS

The Royal Court is available to hire for celebrations, rehearsals, meetings, filming, ceremonies and much more. Our two theatre spaces can be hired for conferences and showcases, and the building is a unique venue for bespoke events and receptions.

For more information, visit
royalcourttheatre.com/events

Sloane Square London, SW1W 8AS ⊖ Sloane Square ⇌ Victoria Station
🐦 royalcourt 📘 theroyalcourttheatre 📷 royalcourttheatre

SUPPORT THE COURT AND BE A PART OF OUR FUTURE.

Every penny raised goes directly towards producing bold new writing for our stages, cultivating and supporting writers in the UK and around the world, and inspiring the next generation of theatre-makers.

You can make a one-off donation by text:

Text **Support 5** to 70560 to donate £5

Text **Support 10** to 70560 to donate £10

Text **Support 20** to 70560 to donate £20

Texts cost the donation amount plus one standard message. UK networks only.

To find out more about the different ways in which you can get involved, visit our website: royalcourttheatre.com/support-us

The English Stage Company at the Royal Court Theatre is a registered charity (No. 231242)

Foreword

Dear reader,

For Black Boys confronts the current crises consuming and confining contemporary Black males, challenging traditional conceptions of Black masculinity and notions of a monolithic, centralised and authentic Black manhood.

The title acknowledges and pays homage to Ntozake Shange's seminal choreopoem *For Colored Girls Who Have Considered Suicide / When the Rainbow Is Enuf*, but while *For Colored Girls* empowers the singular and collective voices of Black women and Black female experiences, *For Black Boys* articulates the heartache, confusion, rage and desires of young Black men. The play explores how the pressures placed on Black men contribute to emotional and mental trauma and the threat of additional Black suicides.

The affirmative resolution of *For Black Boys* is signifying on the collective community of brotherhood that calls for Black men to first love themselves then learn to love one another by recognising the redeeming forces of the king that is within. The underlying issue is that Black males are voiceless and invisible, groomed not to ever show their emotions, groomed into a vision of hyper-masculinity heightened by the media but more so by their own environment.

My hope is to encourage Black male youth to follow their own dreams of finding themselves and aspire to become more than what society expects them to be.

Rest in Eternal Peace, Ntozake Shange, you've inspired a whole generation.

Love and respect, Ryan Calais Cameron

For Black Boys Who Have Considered Suicide When the Hue Gets Too Heavy

Dedicated to Daddy's beautiful boys

Jaiden Cameron
Zechariah Cameron
Ezra Cameron
Josiah Cameron

Characters

Obsidian, *young Black man*
Sable, *young Black man*
Pitch, *young Black man*
Onyx, *young Black man*
Jet, *young Black man*
Midnight, *young Black man*

The sound of a saxophone plays as the boys
begins to rise up and find their own rhythms.

Obsidian
Shake off dark phases of manhood and
the complexities of his complexion

Sable
Expected to grow with no nourishment
no love or no healing

Pitch
Let a Black boy move, let him shake and shuffle without fear

Onyx
Let a Black boy dance, and let him
take up as much space as he needs

Jet
He has been patient turning the other
cheek so much his neck is stiffing up

Midnight
But don't get it twisted, never think he's weak,
his resilience has just been consistent

Onyx
As he rises into his presence and into his persistence
Pitch
Let him step into his promise don't you dare hold him back
his history is no longer in hostage

All of the Boys
AND THIS IS FOR BLACK BOYS WHO
HAVE CONSIDERED SUICIDE WHEN
THE HUE GETS TOO HEAVY

The sound of a school bell goes off.

Pitch
Run!

*The boys all disperse up and down over and under a playful
movement piece. We soon see* **Jet** *standing on his own, centre stage.*

Jet
Age six, playing kiss chase, or should I say *miss-chase*.
I'm over here. Hey! Hi!
These girls are ready for the kill with
stolen lip balm looking greasy
But if Black is beautiful like Mummy told me
Why they all chasing White boy Stephen Pendry?
All us dark-skin boys sat alone in the
middle of the playground.
I'm crying my eyes out.
Stephen picks me up, and says I can run with him
Wow, my hero . . .
Cos this is before I knew White saviour complex was a ting.
His blond curtain-cut hair blowing in my
face like a Poundland Leo DiCaprio.
And these girls are mad fast but they can't catch us though
So much fun being on the run but when
that adrenaline goes . . .
It's clear to see . . .
Weren't no one even chasing me.
That night I go home
Something's gotta be done!
A month ago it was all Tweenies, Teletubbies and Barney
I love you and you love me
I love you but can't love me
Because the gaze in which I see isn't made for me
And I can't negotiate that . . . cos I'm just a baby.
I'm already learning new ways to hate me.
'Mum, why don't girls wanna kiss me?'
She's shocked.
I'm about seven years too early for the birds or bees
'Mum . . . Can I please be White?'

All of the Boys
What?

Jet
Like right now, please can I just be right?

All of the Boys
What?

Jet
Like right now, please can I just be liked?
All I ever wanted
Was to play kiss chase like Stephen Pendry
For them to really want me . . . for me!
Without this curse
The colour Black
Something which I never chose to be
On my skin for all to see, just there haunting me
. . . Why me?

Silence.

Pitch
Ip dip do the doggy did a poo he went to the cinema at
half past two. When the film started, everybody farted, so.
Out. Goes. You. (*Repeated you, you, you.*)

They all seem to close in on **Sable**
*something that started as playful now turns ugly and
the other boys begin aggressively shouting and
chasing down* **Sable** *at pace.*

Sable
I'm age thirteen walking down Mare Street and hear the
sirens go off. A bully-van whizzes past me, PHEW! . . .
Then pulls up at the end of the road.
'Ahh, not today, man'
They open up the door and jump out like flipping
Power Rangers making poses and all sorts.
'STOP, GET ON THE WALL'
And I'm bare confused cos I can't do both innit.
They start asking the usual crap like –

Onyx (*as* **Officer**)
Where are you coming from?

Sable
And –

Obsidian (*as* **Officer**)
Where are you off to?

Sable
Mind your business! 'Bout you wanna ask big man questions.
Come out my flipping face!
. . . That's what I wanted to say . . . but I got new jeans on
and didn't feel to be faced down in the dirt with a man's
knee firmly placed on my neck back.
So, I said 'home' and 'meeting my boys'

Jet (*as* **Officer**)
We're gonna need to search you.

The boys sigh.

Pitch
What did you do?

Obsidian/Midnight/Sable/Onyx/Jet
What?!

Pitch
What did you do for them to search you?

Sable
Erm let me think . . . being guilty of . . . being Black –

Onyx
Between the ages of thirteen and a hundred –

Obsidian
Weighing between seven and eighteen stone –

Jet
And between four foot eight and seven foot eight.
Yea that's about it.

Everyone laughs other than **Pitch**.

Pitch
What did they find?

Sable
What do you mean?! My phone, my wallet, and this (*takes his hands out of his pocket to reveal his middle finger*)
Said it was a 'routine check'

All of the Boys *sing 'Routine Check' by The Mitchell Brothers.*

Pitch
Suppose they're just doing their job though, right?

All of the Boys
WHAT?

Onyx
Should I knock him out? I'll do it you know!

Obsidian
Hear him out.

Midnight
Hear what, fam? They're bullies on a power trip –

Pitch
Gun and knife crime have been on the up, I think we could do with more of an authoritative-slash-police presence –

Onyx
Did he just say 'more police'?
Na sorry, this brudda
is getting knocked out!

Jet
Calm down . . . He might have a point.

Midnight/Onyx/Sable
WHAT?

Onyx
What's going on right now?
Firefighters don't go around looking for fires do they?
Doctors don't go 'round looking for patients do they?

So why the police gotta go 'round looking to arrest people?
If we need them, we'll call them innit!

They boys shout and holler and agree/disagree.

Midnight
I didn't even know Black man believed
in those kinds of things you know.

Onyx
It's these flipping university bruddas innit?

Jet/Obsidian/Pitch
What?

Onyx
Do you go university or not?

Jet
Yea I do but –

Sable
Case closed!

Obsidian
What's that gotta do with –

Onyx
Rolling around with all them White man innit.

All of the Boys
Ahh come on, man

Onyx
Come on what? They're Whitewashing him

Jet
What do you mean Whitewashing?

Onyx
Shit, thought *you* would've known but guess
they Whitewashed your ass too.
Means you go to a White uni, get taught by White
teachers, hang around your White classmates talking
a lot of White shit

Acting like you can really relate but to them
you're still another nigger
Then you graduate, choose to work under a White
employer, feel really good about yourself cos you're the
only nigger working there, the first one the company
has ever had.
Then you go out with your workmates, meet a nice White
girl. You love her, your *Caucasian persuasion*
And she loves you cos you're strong and dark like a nigger
but you went to uni so you talk and act White; mans like
Hovis, she gets the best of both worlds.
Then you get married, have a big White wedding, hardly
invite anyone you used to know cos those days are behind
you now. You no longer relate to the struggle and the
people in it.
You move into your big White house in your small White
community. With these Black kids with their White mum,
neighbourhood, school and friends, crying on your lap
about why they have nigger locks, whilst Katie and Poppy
have long straight good hair
And your wife standing there embarrassed because it's a
world she knows nothing about, and you standing there
embarrassed because it's a world that you have long
'forgotten!
Then one day some shit goes down at the company.
Some theft or fraud or corruption, and guess who's first to
be fitted in the frame?
All this time you thought they were your friends, your
neighbours, your colleagues, you believed that you were
really one of them but to them you've always been a nigger.
Just another nigger, a low-down dirty nigger, and that the
damn truth! –

Obsidian

Bullshit! Not sure who told you that you know me but I can
assure you that you. Don't. Know. Me.
Just because a brother is trying to better himself doesn't
mean he's trying to be White. Just because a brother has an

opinion opposed to your own doesn't mean he's trying to be White. Just because a brother is grammatically correct and trying to get an education doesn't mean he is trying to be White. You wanna know why so many brothers end up leaving the endz and never coming back? Not cos they're 'Whitewashed' you dummy, but because they're tired of having to explain themselves to ignorant brothers like you –

The boys run wild.

Midnight
OHHHHHH

Sable
KABOOOM

Jet
You gonna have that cos I wouldn't have that but think you might have that though

The boys laugh.

Onyx
Whatever, man, just remember no matter whether you come back or not, to them you still a nigger in a coupe.

Obsidian
I ain't a nigger do you hear me?! I don't answer to that name. I don't care if you spell it with an 'a' or an 'er' and I don't care who uses it. I am not a nigger in a coupe, I'm not a nigger in Paris, I'm not your nigga or their nigger, never have been never will be. The word is vile, it's how they referred to us whilst they were beating us on the plantations, or lynching us in the Deep South, or what they used to scream at me in primary school when I got chased home, I didn't know what it meant then, but I knew that I never wanted to be called it again.

Silence.

Midnight
Yo, Doctor Umar, is it really that deep though?
We've given it a new meaning now innit?

Sable
Yea it's like a brotherhood ting!

The boys shout and holler with various opinions.
'Hot N*gga' by Bobby Shmurda begins to play. All of the
boys other than **Obsidian** *break out into the Shmoney dance.*
Obsidian *interrupts the music.*

Obsidian
Of all the words in the English language to unite and
empower us we chose that one? Why not brother, prince,
king? Words have meanings. We lose all self-respect once
we adopt that name . . . Call me what you like but don't
ever call me no nigger. OK?

The boys murmur amongst themselves.

Pitch *steps out alone . . .*

Pitch
I could never use the . . . N word . . . Don't know why.
I never felt comfortable enough. Suppose I never
felt Black enough, weird right? Because . . . I'm clearly
Black . . . right?
I remember 'International Day' at school
and the way I denied my heritage!
I made up that I was from St Kitts or the Virgin Islands
because no one knew anything about those places
And I would have gotten away with it too if my parents
didn't decide to come in full traditional attire with the
gele, agbabda and ice cream tubs full of jollof rice
for the teachers.
It was so embarrassing.

The boys all laugh.

Pitch
By the time I was in secondary all I wanted to do was
read comic books, skateboard, listen to Iron Maiden and be

a teenage dirtbag, baby. I didn't even notice I
was the only Black boy doing it till
my lab partner a White girl named Ruth Woods
sits next to me and says:

Sable (*as* **Ruth**)
I like the fact you don't act Black. You're a
'Oreo', Black on the outside, White on the
inside

Pitch
If I'm not Black, THEN WHAT THE HECK AM I? Like is
there some kind of manual or something?
My only understanding of 'acting Black' was church on
Sundays, being well dressed, good
grades, good job and getting married.
That's what I grew up around. As I dug deeper it seemed to
be this bipolar opposite version of Blackness.
To be Black you have to be ill mannered and
be some kind of big pimp player.
I had this desperate need to black up, before anybody else
noticed. I packed my comic books away and hung up my
skateboard, and started hanging around this
group of Black guys who all listened to the same kind
of

All of the Boys
'Nigger this, nigger that, money clothes and hoes'

Pitch
Music. All spoke in this broken English-Jamaican
patios, despite being from Ghana and Nigeria
And if you dared to be different, you would face the fate of
being ridiculed or, even worse, being
told,

Onyx
You act 'White', you're a sell-out!

Pitch
You say 'I wanna do my homework'

Midnight
Ahhh you're a neek, fam!

Pitch
You don't want to be in a gang, or carry a knife,

Onyx
Ahhh you're moist.

Pitch
It's like I finally found the manual and realised that
I didn't like it. I forced myself, but found that I
couldn't comply. I guess I'm just not Black enough to be
Black

Jet
That hyper-aggressive, hardened, thug-like character has
been accepted as 'Black' not just by the masses, but most
notably by our own community!

Obsidian
Any of you ever feel like it's about time we started being
more responsible for the representation of our people?

Jet
We are not a monolith, and even if we were
by no means should *that* pose as our image.

Sable
Yea but we have to still be 'inclusive' of people like my man
over here who actually live that life! Ahhhaaaa!

Onyx
Suck your mum yea!

The boys burst out laughing.

Obsidian
We need to familiarise ourselves with leaders and role
Models both from our present and our past . . .

The boys agree with hmmms and ummms.

Pitch
Like Black history right? Because –

Midnight
Fuck Black history, man!

All of the Boys
What!

Midnight
You deaf? Man said fuck it!
What good ever came from Black history, bro? How does
teaching a brudda that we used to get beaten in the streets
by little White men gonna empower him? Telling a man that
our ancestors were out there in the flipping field picking
cotton getting their ass beat? How is that empowering? You
tell me innit cos you're looking at me like I'm mad!

Silence.

Midnight
Year Eight, we had Black History Week, not even month,
'week'. They made us watch *Roots*.

The boys all react.

Bro, no context or introduction you know
That film made me sick! Watching all that shit we went
through
I couldn't get my head around why we allowed that to
happen.
I was just sitting there trying not to catch eye contact
with no one.
'Next White boy that even talks to me . . . it's peak for them'
Then little Peter Davidson, blond hair, blue eyes, big
chipmunk cheeks, looked the type that would have had
slavemasters in his ancestry; try ask *me* for a pen?

All of the Boys
OH SNAP

Midnight
What in the caucasity! Must have thought this was slavery
times, boy!
'I ain't gotta give you shit no more!'
Bang! Left hook to the *temple* put man in *prayer* position.
I got detention for the next three days!
Couldn't even tell no one why I really hit him, couldn't
articulate it, didn't have the words or the language
Just thought . . . No one would understand me.
Black history did nothing for me. I was better off not
knowing any of that madness.

Obsidian
I hear you, but you know Black history predates the
transatlantic slave trade right?
Before Africa was robbed, and raped, we had a
rich continent of kings and queens, great warriors,
architecture, education and –

Onyx
Yea, I swear that's one Nas tune though.

Jet
I know I can . . . be what I wanna be

All of the Boys
If I work hard at it, I'll be where I wanna be

Obsidian
You lot know about Tariq ibn Ziyad and the Moorish
invasion of Europe?

The boys look around confused.

Tariq was the general of the Moorish command
from Africa. Tariq was bold, strong, courageous, and
Black! Tariq would stand up to anyone. He was a
mercenary, a military leader who brought down the
Visigoths of Spain with 7,000 of his men against
100,000 of theirs.
Tariq weren't about taking any shit from any White boys

The boys murmur and engage with this subject matter.

He brought such things as paper, and
fruits like oranges, lemons and sugar cane to Europe
for the first time. He was a visionary, a scholar, a mighty
hero. The mightiest
And I wanted to be his friend so bad!

The boys laugh.

Most people had imaginary friends growing up, I had Tariq
ibn Ziyad. We would conquer the sandpit, liberate the
jungle-gym and battle with the bullies in the dinner
hall.
One time Tariq even put Nelson Barnes in a headlock when
he cussed my mum, even though I was the one that got the
blame. He was bold and brave enough to ask Shakira Brown
for a kiss on the cheek, even though I got the pleasure.
Tariq was my first impression of a Black man. I thought all
Black men were Tariq, knew Tariq, or aspired to be Tariq.

Midnight
Hold on, is man saying Spain was Black? Lemme Google
that, cos them things can't be true?

Obsidian
Not just Spain, the Moors went on to conquer the
Iberian Peninsula –

Onyx
Yo, easy on them mad words, big man

Obsidian
So, Portugal, France, Andorra, Sicily, ALL UNDER
AFRICAN RULE

Sable
That's why them Spanish girls got a little chocolate
flake to their vanilla ice cream innit?

The boys all verbally agree.

Pitch
How do you know all that?

Obsidian
I just read a lot.

Jet
Why don't they teach any of that in school though?

Sable
If they taught that in school could you imagine
how bawsy we could be?

Onyx
How that would make a man feel, instead of just hearing
about Henry the Eighth duppying bare wives

Midnight
Certain man would be prouder of their identity innit?

Obsidian
My mum always used to say, 'If you want to hide
something from a Black man put it in a book'

All of the Boys
Ahh what / what she on about? / that ain't true

Obsidian
What's the last book you read?

All of the Boys
Ahh, pssh . . . What? . . .

Obsidian
Just imagine, our ancestors were being killed for
reading, kids nowadays wouldn't read if it killed 'em –

Onyx
Raa, come to think of it, it might have been a Biff and
Chip book you know.

Midnight
Oh my days, remember dat?!

Jet
My father banned those books, said we weren't allowed to
read books with magic in them

The boys laugh.

Dads are mad like that . . . innit?

Silence. The boys turn away or shrug their shoulders.

My father was my hero.

Onyx
My dad was a villain.

Jet
A good man, a man that served his God.

Onyx
A wicked man, a man that on the *right*
day would serve you a *left* hook.

Jet
He loved me, I reminded him of hope.

Onyx
He hated me, I reminded him of himself.

Jet
Growing up I thought of my father as the biggest,
tallest, strongest, smartest, bravest man I
knew. I never saw my father cry he was so
mighty like King T'Chaka of Wakanda!
And I was his Prince T'Challa and we reigned supreme
over the whole household (*laughs*).

Onyx
Growing up I thought of my dad as the biggest,
tallest, strongest, dumbest coward I
knew. Growing up I never saw my father cry. He was
destructive like a wrecking ball and I was the collateral
damage

Jet
He made extreme sacrifices to ensure we had a better
quality of life then he did, to ensure we went to a
good school, had good clothes and always had good food

at the table. As kids my sister and I grew frustrated
at the lack of time he could spend with us. That he was
never at parents' day or at sports day cheering us on.
We had unrealistic expectations of our father. We
expected him to be perfect.

Onyx

He made no effort whatsoever to ensure we had a better
quality of life than he did.
No effort to ensure we went to a good school, had clothes or
food on the table.
He made life harder for my mother not easier.
Growing up me and my little brother grew frustrated at
his sight.
He was a bum, a dead beat, he would never turn up to
things like parents' day or sports day. We had basic
expectations of what a father should be. I expected him to
be a man, make money, not drink away the little he had.
Protect, take an interest and teach me something about
myself.

Jet

Dad came home early from work saying he wanted to talk to
us. Dad never came home early from work unless one of us
needed a 'special beating'
You know those limited
addition beatings that Mum wouldn't give.
Dad never liked giving a beating but when he did give them.
DAMN!
So, my sister and I sat on our dining table
trembling, helping each other go over every naughty
thing we could have possibly done over the last two
years.
We needed to know the reason for this forthcoming
untimely execution.
Dad came in looking physically tired and dishevelled.

Silence . . .

Then he looked up at me, stole my gaze, and he said,
'I've been diagnosed with prostate cancer'.
I didn't know what a prostate was, but I knew cancer could
kill!
My whole world stopped.
'How long have you known?'

Onyx (*as* **Dad**)
. . . three years.

Jet
And you're only telling us now!

Onyx (*as* **Dad**)
Look . . .

Jet
What treatment have you been on?

Silence.

You've had cancer for three years and you haven't had
any treatment? Are you mad?

Onyx (*as* **Dad**)
'Ey, are *you* mad? Have you forgotten that I am your
father, have you forgotten that this is my house?

Jet
I was ragging, I didn't care if I was going to get a beating
I couldn't believe he would do this to us
I stopped but not because he had told me to
But because I was witnessing something that I had never
witnessed in my whole entire life.
. . . My father crying . . .
His tears paralysed me
He told me that this type of cancer attacked the prostate
gland with a particularly high rate in African and
Afro-Caribbean men.
He wasn't the first man in our family to ever have the
disease, but the first to discuss it.

'Why did you take so long to tell us, to get it sorted out?'
He replied a reply that still haunts me to this day . . . He said

Onyx (*as* **Dad**)
Son I had to make a
tough decision, I had to choose between my health and
being a man

Silence.

Jet
My father died in my mother's arms six months later.
He wanted to remain perfect. Immortalised. To exceed our
unrealistic expectations of him.
He believed men who are vocal about any kind of health
issues
can be dismissed as weak. As inferior. Broken guys
who are more likely to be ostracised for their honesty
instead of rewarded for their bravery.
He needed to be 'manly' so much that he would sacrifice his
whole life for it.
I wonder if only he knew he was *enough* just the way he was
. . . would he still be here?

Silence.

Onyx
Now you need to understand my father never came home
early cos he was always at the bookies till they chucked him
out.
Then he'd be at the pub till they'd chuck him out.
Mum worked two jobs so she would come home late and
sometimes not at all.
But one evening my father came home early.
I remember the sound of the door slamming and hearing
him stumbling across the corridor.
I remember that feeling it started in my throat and worked
its way through my chest down to my arse.
I literally thought I was going to shit myself.
I looked at my little brother Aaron miming,

'WHAT THE FUCKING FUCK ARE WE GOING TO DO?'
He tries to run
I grab him –

Sable (*as* **Aaron**)
We're in too deep, bro, I'm out

Onyx
What do you mean 'you're out'? You little waste-man

Sable (*as* **Aaron**)
I mean I'm going to bed. I'm gonna pretend I was
sleeping the whole time

Jet (*as* **Dad**)
Aaron! Is that you making a whole leap of noise?

Sable (*as* **Aaron**)
No, Dad, I'm asleep! I've been asleep all night!

Onyx *slaps* **Aaron** *at the back of his head.*

Jet (*as* **Dad**)
Get here now!

Onyx
Aaron went out to meet Dad, and I turned around heading
for the stairs. I was home free no beating for me!
Every step I took I could hear Aaron's beats getting louder
I couldn't walk any further
The beatings were too much
This wasn't discipline this was a man possessed
He was gonna kill Aaron.
'STOP!'

Jet (*as* **Dad**)
Don't worry fool, you' next.

Onyx
I said stop yea!

Jet (*as* **Dad**)
You turn badman now?

Onyx
Bada-man than you.

Jet (*as* **Dad**)
'Ey, are you mad? Have you forgotten that I am your
father, have you forgotten that this is my house?

Onyx *punches his dad in the face knocking him to the ground,*
BANG!

Onyx
I hate you I hate you I hate you!

He mimes beating down on his father's face.

I hit him! I hit him, I hit my dad.
He's tryna get back up. I hit him again, and again, I just kept
beating on him
I beat his ass, I beat him like a baby, mashed him like
potatoes!
He was finished.
That was the day I dethroned the king to become a king
That was the day I truly became a man.
Cos any pussy with a dick can have a child but it takes a real
man to raise a man and he weren't no fucking man!

Silence.

I would have thought my mum would have been pleased
But she loved that nigga more than us and I never
understood that shit.

Silence.

My loyalties now gravitated towards men of rebellion
Towards brotherhood, towards man-dem because who needs
to be raised by a man, when you can be dragged up by
man-dem!
To hell with suffering. To hell with pain. To hell with
helplessness.
We would be liberated and find paradise by our own names.
You would call us a gang but if you spoke to me before you

spoke about me, or even worse, for me, you would know we
spoke in the same tongue

All of the Boys
Our brother's keepers

Onyx
They taught me what it meant to survive, on unfertile land
that spits out Black boys whole.
Taught me how to make kingdoms out of sand cos you done
took all our gold.
Taught me how to outsmart death, cheat him and make it
out day by day on these roads.
Taught me what it means to be a badman, cos good men die
young and young men die feeling old in the land of
forgotten souls.
A badman knows how to preserve life, and ain't afraid to
take a life.
Knows how to live a life
because if you a true badman life is on your side it's fucking
scared not to be!

All of the Boys
A child that is not embraced by the village will burn it down
to feel its warmth

*Kendrick Lamar's 'The Blacker the Berry' drops, the boys begin to
huddle around* **Onyx** *like members of his gang, letting out all of
their pain and hurt and rage, then the song fades out, the boys
exhausted.*

*The mood and the music suddenly change to Ghost Town DJ's 'My Boo'.
The boys are looking all innocent and coy.*

Interval.

All of the Boys *sing Blackstreet's 'No Diggity'.*

Sable
It's like every time I get a
New girl, it's like getting a gold medal.
Feels like I'm winning.
At first it was just about getting the body count up
Letting brothers know that I could get more than you get on
a slow day.
Then that became too easy
Obviously, I've been light-skin'd my whole life
so women are naturally attracted to me

The boys start shouting abuse in disagreement.

You heard of White privilege; you ever heard of Peng
privilege?

The boys start shouting abuse in disagreement again.

So, I started challenging myself with different areas, races,
even older women
I'm the brother that has grown men's mummies calling me
Daddy – I'm a bad boy.
I realised that every woman loves chocolate, you get me?

The boys agree.

Especially that Caramel Crunch.

The boys laugh.

The first time my boys heard about my exploits was the first
time I was ever called 'a man'.
No one ever taught me about manhood
But I felt 'pussy' certified that for me.
Feeling like the universe made me for women, like that was
my purpose, like I was chiselled and crafted by Zeus'
lightning bolt

All the Boys
Pow!

Sable
What'd you know about me?

All of the Boys
Pow!

Sable
I'm lethal with the D!

The boys laugh.

Men would respect me, and women would fall in
love with me, want me and need me, and I loved that.
I loved being more than just . . . I suppose being more than
just a regular nigga, you get me?
Then these girls would tell me about
their thoughts, and emotions and shit, and
I tell myself that it's OK to leave before the sun
rises because she could never really understand me
anyway . . .
She can't really love *me* right?
And what if she does and expects me to love her back?
I'm young, Black and from endz
Us-man are not worthy of all of that.
So I shy away, start taking long to reply to her WhatsApps
emotionless whenever she calls
Then eventually just lock her off.
Now I feel like a boy again, starving, out on the prowl in
need of my next fix
Because without my boys breading me, and without the
women begging me, how could I truly be a man . . . right?

The boys nod in agreement.

But I slyly hope things are different with this *new* girl. I
actually like her . . . bare!
Last night I stayed over at hers and something different
happened, like I stayed all the way till breakfast

All the Boys
What?

Sable

I'm telling you and I could have stayed all morning if it
weren't chest and leg day

All the Boys
What?

Sable *sings the chorus to 'Last Night' by Az Yet.*

Sometimes I have dreams about her but not like dirty
dreams but dreams with clothes on and stuff.
When she talks to me . . . like . . . I listen

The boys jump up shouting and hollering in disbelief.

Like she's actually making sense and that . . . and I know
bare things about her too, like her last name,
and her cat's name, and her birthday.
We do cute stuff like picnics, and stargazing, but it doesn't
even feel cute, it feels . . . slyly badman!

Onyx
Slyly nothing, man, this is some fruity shit!

Pitch
Will you just let the boy finish?!

Sable
I mean it feels pretty good but I know how these things go
I'll keep holding off commitment
And she'll get tired of waiting and call time on my foothold
stop letting me use her pussy for a pillow
And I'll smile, and hide the pain of knowing that she wants
me to be her *man*, but soon enough I'll feel like a *boy* again,
in need of another fix
I feel to tell her how I'm feeling but don't tell a soul
Full to brim with fake confidence
Don't show or you've failed the show
Man up!
Like, what would the man-dem say?
'Another girl, another day'

And I deny myself of love . . . But I don't know how long I can continue this way . . .

Pitch
Are you in love? –

Onyx
Blackman don't fall in love! Don't try put ideas in his head!

Jet
You do know how dumb that sounds right?

Obsidian
Nothing wrong with falling in love it –

Onyx
Don't exist, it's just some Illuminati ting –

Jet
What?!

Onyx
To try and make people buy shit they don't need.

Obsidian
Let me tell you from experience, ain't nothing more manly than being faithful, and committed to one woman –

Midnight
Ahhh shut up, man, what do you know!

Obsidian
I have a woman, you fool

All of the Boys
WHAT!

Obsidian
Why are you so surprised? About six months now.

All of the Boys
WHAT!

Midnight
Why you are keeping it on the down low? She look like
Quasimodo or something?

Obsidian
She's beautiful actually, and bold, and intelligent –

Onyx
Whatever, man! Where she from?

Midnight
Yea like where's she from-from?

Obsidian
Ghanaian

Midnight
And?

Obsidian
And what?

Onyx
Ghanaian and what? What is she mixed with?
Stop playing dumb, fam.

Obsidian
She's straight Ghanaian. She isn't mixed!

Midnight and **Onyx** *share a glance of disbelief.*

Obsidian
Hold on are you telling me a Black woman's beauty should
derive from the non-black part of her?
Please remember that neither of your mothers are
'mixed' so –

Midnight
Whoa, calm down, no one ain't saying that, bro

Onyx
You ain't gotta get mums involved

Midnight
A lot of people like their coffee with a little swirl of milk.

Obsidian
Not me. I like my coffee black, natural and 100 per cent
African!
I drank her in, and I was not thirsty. I tasted her glory, her
grace and her power
I love her.
She's my Isis, a goddess reincarnate.
One gaze at her beauty, and my soul surrenders.
Her natural hair stimulates the conscious acknowledgement
of her perfection.
Her skin is smooth like silk, soft as the finest Egyptian
cotton.
Her complexion as wonderful as the rarest cocoa bean.
She has that brown skin

All of the Boys *sing the bridge to 'Brown Skin' by India Arie.*

Obsidian
She makes me want to inhale her, and fill myself with the
overwhelming infestation of her beauty.
She's my queen! And her love is second to none.
I'm telling you there is nothing greater than the love of a
beautiful Black woman.

Silence.

Jet
Mad. I thought you were into White girls . . .

The boys burst out laughing and hollering.

Pitch
What if her looks fade? Beauty is vanity not love. The Bible
says love should be patient, kind, it doesn't envy,
it's not boastful, proud, selfish or easily angered.
You haven't mentioned any of those qualities. You've
basically said, 'I love her because she looks good to me'

Silence.

Onyx
Your head hurting?

Obsidian
What?

Onyx
Cos man just fell off that high horse innit

The boys burst out laughing and hollering.

Obsidian
How you know so much about love anyway?

Pitch
What?

Onyx
You ever been with anyone, like anyone?

Pitch
Don't worry . . . just know that I'm doing me.

Onyx
We know you're doing you. We're trying to
find out if you're doing anyone else?

The boys laugh.

Remember in school when people were like, 'Yea I've
got a girlfriend but she just don't go to this school'

The boys start laughing.

You still a virgin?

Pitch
What?

Sable
Leave it now

Onyx
Don't act like you didn't hear me.

Pitch *getting really awkward.* **Midnight** *steps in.*

Midnight (*to* **Onyx**)
Are *you* though?

Onyx
Are you mad? Man was like fifteen or something

Jet
I was seventeen!

Sable
Seventeen?! Wait . . . That means (*counts fingers*) you went
the whole of school without popping the Pringles? What the
hell were you going for?

Jet
To get an education, bro

Sable
Ahh yea-yea, that's decent.

Obsidian
I must have been fourteen

Sable
Same, I felt old to lose it at fourteen though.
Think I was a bit scared

Midnight
Of pussy?

Sable
Of catching something or the condom
slipping off, you get me?

All of the Boys
Hmm . . . Yea, man!

Sable
Or even . . . not measuring up to a girl's expectations . . .

Onyx
Ahh yea, true-say you're only half Black innit?

The boys all laugh.

Sable
Dickhead!

Midnight
You man were late bloomers, man . . . I was nine

All of the Boys
Nine!

Jet
Seriously?

Midnight
Yea, man! . . . What?

Silence.

I'm a veteran out here, a beast you know what I'm saying?

Silence.

Apart from this one time . . .

Pitch
Go on

Midnight
. . . No, man, I'm talking too much talk

Sable
Ain't that what we are here to do?

Midnight
You lot are acting weird

Onyx
Go-tru, bro, no judgement

Midnight
. . . This one time . . . one time . . . man, I just (*flops his hand*)

All of the Boys
Ooooowwwww

Midnight
Couldn't get the big man moving for nothing . . . just froze
It's the first time staying over at my girl's and she's trying

her best, doing funky stuff, like candles, and incense and
music, even spent mad money on expensive lingerie which I
always find crazy, don't mean I don't like it, I just mean after
I've seen it
I ain't tryna see it if you know what I'm saying . . .
I'm ready, stripped down to my Pri-marnis
I ain't playing
Then the song skips to

'At Your Best' by Aaliyah begins to play.

I just freeze! She's mad understanding, more understanding
than I care to understand
Asking me if I want a cuddle and that.
Na, man, I wanna know why something is happening to me
that has never happened to me before, and I'm making sure
she knows that.
The song instantly takes me back to being eight or nine at
Mum's house with my cousins
Man, it was the best of times. Martha was a couple years
older, so she was in charge, like an aunty but way cooler
Martha let us stay up later than 8.30 on a school night!
Just as long as we didn't say nothing to no one
And on weekends we used to watch that movie with those
big scary worm mutherfuckers that come out the ground
if you make noise
We used to watch that whole damn movie in silence, ain't no
one move for shit, it ain't worth it man . . .
Martha had to sleep on the sofa and she would always put
Aaliyah on when she had a boyfriend over, right before they
would begin to take off their clothes and do grown people shit
The music mused me as I lay back in bed and think about
what it would be like if someone thought a brudda like me
could be pretty enough to call 'baby'.
If someone could love me as deep as the people in these love
songs?

The beat skips.

One night I saw the big scary worms in my nightmares
worms jumping out at me from the wardrobe and beneath
the bed
Martha enters the room asking if I'm scared? . . .
I ain't no chicken, no baby, I ain't afraid of no worm
monsters and I ain't afraid of no grown people stuff either.
I try to keep my head in the music
Take me away if only for three minutes
and forty-seven seconds
Having someone love on my body without me there
loving on my body without me being there but I could still
feel it
and it hurt, and some nights I still feel it
and I never wanna feel that way again if that's what love feels
like.
And I'm tryna articulate it to my mum but I'm tripping on
my words, like a foreigner who hasn't mastered the language.
So she just tells me it's all in my head
cos Martha comes for free and she's doing her best
so it's literally all she can afford.
And I can see you lot looking at me like a victim but I mean I
was . . . hard . . . the whole time, a man can't get that way less
he's into it right?

All of the Boys
No!
My body is my body for me
My body won't keep your lies
My body won't keep your promises
My body won't keep your secrets
Your body is your body for you, bro, and nobody can take
that away from you

These words are really beginning to affect **Midnight**.

Midnight
I don't always know how to touch or want to be touched or
know how to want someone to touch me, and only trust
people when they have proven to me that they can be

trusted. And not even the Queen Aaliyah can save me now,
cos all her voice does is remind me of a time when death laid
over me
I would wish that he would take me by night and save me
from another day, because I literally felt like no one else
would.

Silence.

All of the Boys *sing the bridge of 'Beautiful' by
Snoop Dog and 'To Midnight' by Pharrell Williams.*

Onyx (*to* **Pitch**)
So you a virgin for real yea?

All of the Boys
Ahhh shut up / leave it now

Pitch
I had a fling last month actually!

All of the Boys
. . . A fling!?

Jet
Sorry, brother, 1998 called, and they want their word
back.

The boys laugh.

Pitch
Hey, excuse me . . . dear beautiful lady that I stand next to
on the train each morning
I know I look really creepy when I look at you but seriously
I'm not a creep.
And just so you know I'm not a baller or a shot-caller.
And I know I don't look like a rapper or those male models
from the music videos
I'm not a freak in the streets and I'm definitely not a freak
between the sheets, and I'm pretty sure my dick game is
incredibly weak, and I hope we'll cross that bridge together
some day . . .

but for now
I just wanted to say . . .
I wonder how you have the cheek to be so beautiful even
though this English weather is so terrible.

The boys mock **Pitch**.

Sable
You should have said
'Aside from being sexy, what do you do for a living?'

Jet
'Hey, my name's Microsoft. Can I crash at your place
tonight?'

Obsidian
'Do you like raisins? How do you feel about a date?'

Onyx
'Well, here I am. What are your other two wishes?'

Midnight
'Did your licence get suspended for driving me crazy?'

All of the Boys
'I was blinded by your beauty; I'm going to need your name
and phone number for insurance purposes.'

The boys burst out laughing.

Pitch
I knew I needed to speak to her but didn't know how. I
asked my pastor and he said,

Jet (*as* **Pastor** *with a Nigerian accent*)
It is not good that the *man* should be alone
If you like her, then tell her. Are you not *man*?

Pitch
I saw her the next day with her hair tied up
She had a heart-shaped head.
I was like, 'My Jesus, this is a sign, oh'
So, I shuffled over to her and said . . .

The boys all stare attentively . . .

. . . Hey . . .

All of the Boys
Ahh, man, what/come on, man

Pitch
She laughs and replies . . .
'Hey'
And I froze, I melted, I froze and melted at the same time
I know it's not possible, but it happened.
'What are you doing Saturday, I would love to know if we
could . . . link up? . . . PLEASE?'

All of the Boys
Ahhh, come on, man!

Jet
I told you 'bout these 1998 terms!

Pitch
She smiled and replied.

Obsidian (*as* **Chloe**)
Oh, I'm busy this Saturday.

Pitch
Oh, no I meant next Saturday.

Obsidian (*as* **Chloe**)
I'm kinda gonna be busy every Saturday.

Pitch
Oh. OK yea well have a nice life.

I got shut down just like that.
I should have never said 'link up'
It's my usual stop I'm about to leave and she taps my
shoulder with a piece of paper in her hand and says

Obsidian (*as* **Chloe**)
I babysit on Saturdays but let's talk. I'll be free again during
the half-term.

Pitch

Hip-hip-hallelujah! I knew her heart-shaped head was a
sign. I snatched that number out her hand, stared at it the
whole way home. 07937775380. I knew it off by heart . . .
But still couldn't call it.
I mean, I wanted to. Just couldn't.
What would I say?
After three days of torturing myself, I wrote down a list of
general conversation starters like
What does your name mean? What is your favourite day of
the week? What do you mean you don't like cheese, I love
cheese! I punch the number in, and wait, it rings out.
I put my phone down and think,
'Oh well, at least I tried'.
Then the phone rings back! 'Chloe xx' on the caller ID!

The boys shout and make noises of celebration.
Pitch *shushes the boys so he can answer the phone.*

Chloe, eh? So, what does your name mean?
She asked me what was up with that random-ass question,
and we laughed.
I eased up, and that's how things remained.
We spoke about Christ, and how we felt his second coming
was upon us. We spoke about cosmetology, the space-time
continuum, and all its apparent dimensions.
We spoke about comics, even though she was DC, and I was
Marvel. I love her
It's perfect, we're perfect . . . too perfect?
And I begin to worry, feeling like I can't stop *worrying*, at the
thought that she's worrying about us or about me, or that
bad things that will happen if I stop worrying about her or
about we.
Truth is that sooner or later she will come to the realisation
that she's just too good for me, right? And she'll need a love
that is less complicated, that leaves her warm and fuzzy and
not exhausted and exasperated
And she'll be right, because she's incredible, and deserves to
be.

I'm afraid that she will only break my heart, but I've grown
so accustomed to nourishing myself in pain that I'm afraid
deep down inside I might actually want her to

Hey, excuse me . . . dear beautiful lady that I stand next to
on the train and stare at each morning . . . I . . . I . . . I wish I
had the courage to talk to you

Jet

As I move through the alley way, I see that sunset that comes
sometimes before the sun sets.
The purple sky that looks like it's been painted on and you
can only look and hope that one day you can dance your
dance under a sky like that.
But not tonight
I'm forced to wait out till dark to move in the dark with my
dark skin to dance my dark dance
In dark places looking for dark people with even darker
secrets
Letting my lusts and passions off the leash like a sniffer dog
searching for that forbidden fruit.
I'm playing with fire, and I know it.
And just like that . . . there you are
And I know I came to do something dark-dark today but
I surrender to your talent and your charm
Every move has flicking tongues on every side
You are the life of the dance a demigod in your prime and
by the time it was dark-dark you would have selected which
dancer would be as a lamb to your altar.
We came to worship you.
I knew more about how your body moved then I knew my
own
We wait burning, sweating, thirsty, hot, bright and eager
A wildfire catching fire catching my eyesight
me . . . Oh shit . . . OK?
With a glance you set my heart ablaze
Take your time with me, move with me into
this fiery rapture, of lost bodies on lost bodies
I moved to your music and found my own rhythm

I felt home touch my chest and wrap its arms around my
waist
I felt safety in your presence and belonging in your pride.
You looked at me, looked at me like I were a man . . . but not
any man, a full man complete, and I hold on tight cos I
never want this song to end
Fearful that when the music stopped
I would go home alone and hide behind the sounds of
Sunday school music.
So, let Carlos play that Spanish guitar till his fingers bleed
And you, you danced as though you wanted us to be seen
And acknowledged that we were here
and we could dance!

Carlos Santana Spanish guitar plays.
Then it slows into 'Happens' by Sampha.

As the music slows and light pours in
I hide my presence and protect my heart.
I take two steps back, let's just hold it whilst we have it.
And time stands still for no man but we were more than men
so for us it'll move slow as if we were watching a memory
stuck in a moment and hoped that it could stay that way.
picture perfect.
But it doesn't matter how it feels it could never be real . . .
Because what you seek
I can't afford not to hide
Products of a culture that deems hetero-masculinity as a
Black man's primary responsibility
And homosexuality as a White man's perversion.
To me the dark represents the safest place to be
I don't risk losing my ties to family, friends and my Black
community.
Being Black is hard enough; being Black and queer can
seem a cruel and impossible proposition
And that's enough for you to carry for your damn self
without my Black ass heavying the load
But I guess that's shit you already know because if you were

truly allowed to be proud you wouldn't be out living and
dying in these shadows

The music stops playing and an instrumental for 'Happens' by
Sampha begins to play.

I apologise for leading you into a tango that I won't be able
to materialise.
So, until a time when we feel free to dance our dance under
purple skies. The ones that look like they've been painted on
. . . we'll continue to only dance in the deepest depth of our
shadows . . . and will continue to shine . . .
even in dark

Onyx *grabs* **Jet** *and holds him; the two men share a moment.*

Onyx
I ain't got no love. This one time this girl try teef all of it
Girl! You better give me back alla my love I don't play!
On Insta thirst-trapping 'bout how you like
Backwards cowgirl
But those were my rides and glides strokes and slides
I gave you those moves and groves slips and tricks
For me for us for we!
Your seasonings, your Scotch bonnet, rosemary, your thyme,
that Reggae Reggae sauce that you think I like, it's still mine
Even though you now feed it to another brother that
reminds you of me but less complicated
I got news for you
Taking my love don't mean it's yours, it means it's stolen!
So I want it back!
Like there seriously needs to be some type of law against
taking someone's love and just expecting them to get on fine
without it.
I downed my barriers for you
Let you into my secrets, spent time with my insecurities
And now you all the way in and you can choose to call upon
my soul any and every time you need a little trick or treat
All you have to do is knock . . .
And I keep letting you in cos I'm desperate . . . to be wanted,

to be looked at, thought of, to laugh with someone and feel
like there's one person in this world that has your back
And look I know Black boys ain't supposed to need love . . .
But I didn't know that till the world taught that
Fleeing from me like the plague, like
my overwhelming blackness must be contagious.
See how many faces turn drastically to fear, in my
presence
Locking car doors as I pass, hiding their
their wallets, their phones, their
manners, their smiles from me.
I must be less than human, right?
Living on road keeps your mind on the risk of an untimely
death
But in my case perhaps it's not soon enough
Cos being alive and being a man, a big Black man, is a
contradiction I haven't quite conquered yet
. . . And the weight of it is crushing me.
Fuck love, man . . .
Fuck a feeling that I no longer believe in
Fuck both night-time and mornings they only good for
grieving
Fuck a heart tear it out burn it chef it's broken and I don't
fucking need it
Fuck air, man, I'm so tired of breathing!
I don't care! Have it. Take all my love!
I'm a soldier, born alone, and I'll die alone,
I'm a man a badman strong Black man.

The boys huddle around **Onyx** *and hold him as he cries.*

You ever feel like Black boys were made to give more love
than we could ever receive?

All of the Boys *sing the chorus to 'Only You' by 112
then sing the chorus to 'Beautiful Girls' by Sean Kingston.*

Obsidian
I remember growing up with Marcus and Anton. Anton was
rough, just a big rough guy. You go to spud him, and you'll

get friction burn. And Marcus was of those side ways-hence
brothers. The ones that stopped growing vertically at twelve
so just banged out gym and grew horizontally instead
They were the baddest, badmen I knew.

Jet (*as* **Marcus**)
Remember Keisha's party?

Midnight (*as* **Anton**)
Even-skin Keisha?

All the Boys
Even-skin Keisha you know?!

Obsidian
Damn! That skin was even!
She was a year above, so majority of the time she acted as
though I didn't exist. Maybe I could change that, because
she was having a house party, and I was invited.

Midnight (*as* **Anton**)
Real girls were gonna be there!

Obsidian
Girls like Pucker-lips Porsche

Jet (*as* **Marcus**)
Bemi with the baby hair, got me going goo goo, gaa gaa

Midnight (*as* **Anton**)
But obviously, wherever real girls are, real guys will follow.

Obsidian
Tough guys, real hench and mean guys,
gangsters even!
But we didn't have to worry about all that cos I was rolling
with Marcus and Anton.
Badmen!

'Party Hard' by Donae'o begins to play.

We're smashed out of our faces on K cider

Jet (*as* **Marcus**)
The boys to girls ratio is ten-to-a-half, not ten-to-one, but ten-to-a-half, and Even-skin Keisha already had ten guys around her fighting for her attention.

Obsidian
But that cheap cider had hit hard and my Dutch courage had kicked in on blast! So, I make my way over. See if I can drop one two bars

Gyptian's 'Hold You' begins to play.

Midnight (*as* **Anton**)
Then door swings open

Obsidian
BANG

Midnight (*as* **Anton**)
It's them boys from Fairfield Estate! A whole squad of them.

Obsidian
And they are watching us watching them watching us but I ain't here to be watching man, I got big plans, I'm here to buss one, two, sweet whines with one, two, sweet ones, or maybe three or four you know . . .

Jet (*as* **Marcus**)
The boys roll in strut through the crowd like they own the place, moving in slow motion. I alert my guys that things might need to get done.

Obsidian
Now common sense would have us run or at least back out gracefully, it's been a good night, good vibes, no sweet whines, but we're young, there's other times, but adrenaline, pride, cheap cider and little Black boys are a well-known cocktail for disaster.

Jet (*as* **Marcus**)
'Oi, pussy'

Obsidian
. . . And I realise we won't be going with common sense
tonight.

Midnight (*as* **Anton**)
Them man are now coming over at pace.

Obsidian
Looking like the Four Horsemen of the Apocalypse
Every stride they take is looking one stride closer to my
Judgement Day.
Marcus and Anton don't look like a single bead of sweat has
been broken between them. I stand there trying to compose
myself feeling like I'm about to vomit, trying to emulate my
boys!
But I can't and I start thinking maybe I'm just not big
enough, bad enough, Black enough for this kind of
altercation. Yea, man, maybe I'm just a different type of
Black
Maybe I got some kind of inactive melanin or something.
Maybe I should let the guys know and just sidestep out. I'm
gonna do that it feels right . . .

Midnight (*as* **Anton**)
When this first one reaches here just give him a swift
uppercut yea?

Obsidian
Why me? You sure about this? Maybe we should just pack –

Midnight (*as* **Anton**)
Him in? Yea pack him in! Good thinking!

Jet (*as* **Marcus**)
Maybe even a little jab, jab, then we got this.

Midnight (*as* **Anton**)
Just aim for the jaw

Jet (*as* **Marcus**)
Yea spin his jaw, blud

Obsidian
I don't know, guys

Jet (*as* **Marcus**)
Do it now, bruv! –

Midnight (*as* **Anton**)
MAN UP! Handle your business, rock his jaw.

All of the Boys
NOW! –

Obsidian
BOOM! In his face left uppercut rocked his flipping jaw!
It was like a cradle in the wind, straight lullaby tings.
His whole crew stepped back. Yea! They better.
Marcus, Anton and I made a run for it, full speed through
the crowd pushing our way past, oh if only Keisha could see
me now. We were buzzing off adrenaline. We ran, but we
didn't lose. We won! I looked to the side of me and saw the
happiness on my boys' faces, they were proud of me. Maybe
I could be a badman! I just didn't know it. I just needed an
event to manifest my inner badman, and now he's here, live
and kicking, and rocking jaws. I wondered what badman
stuff I would do next!

Onyx (*as* **Gang Leader**)
You lot think you're bad yea?!

Obsidian
Hmm . . .The brother I just knocked out seems to have
gained consciousness.

Onyx (*as* **Gang Leader**)
Now what, you lot wanna go again yea, cos I'm in the mood
to be knocking niggas out all over the place

Obsidian
Every man steps up, eye to eye, mirror image.
He who fights with monsters should be careful lest he
thereby become a monster. And if thou gaze long into an
abyss, the abyss will also gaze into thee.

*Looking anywhere but ahead . . . then locks eyes with the gang
leader; it's painful.*

I step forward ready

Jet (*as* **Marcus**)
So does the bruddah with the bright coco on his head, he's
ready. We're

All of the Boys
(*breathe*)
Ready

Obsidian
Wait guys actually . . .

Jet (*as* **Marcus**)
Bang!

Obsidian
Out of nowhere Anton pulls out a six-inch blade and decides
to plunge it into the guy's abdomen. Then he twisted it, he
twisted the blade so the wound wouldn't close an image I will
never be able to erase.
Believe me I have tried.
I stood there amongst the chaos watching litres of blood
leave this boy, like a dam holding up Black boys' futures had
burst at the seams. Anton twisted that blade without a single
thought, for this boy's father, mother, his sisters and
brothers, for his teachers and mentors, for the kids he never
got to seed for the dreams he dreamed and could have
dreamed, for the man he was and could have been. He
dropped straight into my arms, I went down to the ground
with him, both scared shitless. I held on to him like this
somebody must mean something to somebody, so we gotta
keep his body alive
I screamed out 'HELP' into the distance to no avail, and
nobody came for us, till they did.

He begins to cry.

By the time the paramedics got here I had so much
blood on me they didn't know which one of us was
the casualty. I couldn't speak, so we were both taken
into the back of an ambulance.
He said his name was Kwame, that he's just a younger,
only wanted to prove that he could roll with the olders,
that he was fourteen, and that his mother would kill him,
if they didn't save him, so please try . . .
He started crying out for his mum, his mother, his *maame*,
crying for his mum like a baby. A badman crying for his
mum like a child?
And in that moment, it occurred to me that 'Mother' is the
name for 'God' in the hearts and mouths of all children . . .
He wasn't no badman, he was a fucking child . . . a little lost
child returning home and searching for the language of the
angels
A little lost child . . . saying his final prayers.
I sat there shivering in silence, thinking that there has to be
more fulfilment to life than just staying alive.
You ever looked deep into a scared Black boy's eyes?
They'll show you what hell looks like
living life with death by his side
self-medicating with false ego and pride
Tussling with his mirror image, He's found no value in it
So often suicide becomes blurred with homicide.
Look him in the eye just one time, I dare you.

Pitch
Dear lovers and motherfuckers
To those who never cared, never spoke, probably never
knew my name.
Your withheld hellos and how are yous did more hurt than
any name calling.
Dear aunties and uncles, at my funeral please don't
come with your
'If only heaven had a phone'
cos I've had one the last ten years and your ass never called.
Dear teachers, I lived in a community that may not be

getting bombed but could be considered war-torn and we ain't getting the care or the therapy, but you continue to be on my neck about why I'm lacking focus today, or two weeks late on my Chemistry. Miss, if you only knew that I've got to overcome a whole entire world, including myself, just before I enter your classroom.

Pastor, you say 'pray, son' but it's hard to open your mouth and pray to a saviour for saving when you're tired, and you don't wanna be saved.
The pleasures of Earth are overrated.
Yours truly
The Black boy you never knew

Sable
Paramedics turn up and I'm struggling to articulate it
Eleven years of education and nobody ever
taught it.
Cognitive constriction is what they call it
And in that *moment*
I thought it was the only way out. Which dispels the myth that suicide is for the weak or selfish; cos in that state, all of those traits are fucking irrelevant, but if you can stand to wait the moment *will* pass

All of the Boys
If you can stand to wait, the moment *will* pass

Jet
I remember it was cold because I had this big, puffy coat on,
I have this vision of me falling to the ground with these
bloody feathers. They saved me
I chose a method with a high fatality rate because I hated the idea that I might actually survive and I would need to ask for help and . . . shit . . . I suppose I'm more like my father then I cared to know

Midnight
I have low-level dread running through my head, so my social media feeds are riddled with memes offering abstract

advice, like: 'Are you ready for a miracle in your life?'
Images of sunsets and silhouettes of people in
complicated yoga positions and it looks like a cool
place to be but not a place for someone like me,
someone who has seen the shit I've seen

Onyx

I've seen mothers lose their sons lose their hope.
I've seen the struggle make people lose their minds.
I've seen desperation make people sell their possessions
sell your possessions, sell their pussy, sell their soul.
I've seen family and friends who raised you
to be like Jesus turn on your ass like Judas.
I've seen sickle cell, diabetes, cancer, AIDS.
I've seen hell. I swear, man, I've seen it all
out here . . . and nothing's
Brought tears to my eyes, like looking into my mother's,
and knowing even she saw nothing here to love . . .
There's a line between not wanting to live
anymore and wanting to die

A loud bang goes off.

Obsidian

And whilst I lay unconscious, I began to dream.
For a few moments I floated, completely calm,
and I no longer hated having to exist.
Like a crow who smells hot blood
you came flying to pull me out
of a glowing stream. And the voice of my mother, and
her father and his mother's father's mother's scream

All of the Boys

For I know the plans I have for you. They are plans for good
and not for disaster, to give you a future and a hope
Your *life* matters but you gotta be living to live our wildest
dreams

Sampha's 'Can't Get Close' instrumental plays out.

Jet
A place where we brown-skinned golden boys
can get close enough to the sun to kiss it.

Midnight
No Caspers or Karens, no cops or no ops
on the block trying to clip our wings so we
all the way up, and we stay there.

Pitch
We stay there, beautiful and Black without spot or blemish
living unapologetically. Made in the image of God

Onyx
Being called back to my body but not
in a casket or a tomb or a shell . . .
A home. A temple. A sanctuary.
I take a moment to just . . . breathe . . .
and feel the heaviness leave
and I release myself from the versions
of me you created to survive your fear

Sable
I release myself from the versions
of me I created to stay alive.

Obsidian
And now I see God in you, and you in me
I see a king in you.

Jet
And God said love your enemy

Pitch
and I obeyed and loved myself . . .

All of the Boys
And this is for Black boys who have considered suicide but
decided that our stories must be told and our joy forever
rising and our strength as much as our vulnerability has got
to be as strong as our ancestors'

For a complete listing of
Methuen Drama titles, visit:

www.bloomsbury.com/drama

Follow us on Twitter and keep up to date
with our news and publications

@MethuenDrama